ISBN 978-0-259-87812-4
PIBN 10827751

1 MONTH OF
FREE
READING

at

www.ForgottenBooks.com

By purchasing this book you are eligible for one month membership to ForgottenBooks.com, giving you unlimited access to our entire collection of over 1,000,000 titles via our web site and mobile apps.

To claim your free month visit:

www.forgottenbooks.com/free827751

English
Français
Deutsche
Italiano
Español
Português

www.forgottenbooks.com

Mythology Photography **Fiction**
Fishing Christianity **Art** Cooking
Essays Buddhism Freemasonry
Medicine **Biology** Music **Ancient**
Egypt Evolution Carpentry Physics
Dance Geology **Mathematics** Fitness
Shakespeare **Folklore** Yoga Marketing
Confidence Immortality Biographies
Poetry **Psychology** Witchcraft
Electronics Chemistry History **Law**
Accounting **Philosophy** Anthropology
Alchemy Drama Quantum Mechanics
Atheism Sexual Health **Ancient History**
Entrepreneurship Languages Sport
Paleontology Needlework Islam
Metaphysics Investment Archaeology
Parenting Statistics Criminology
Motivational

DEVOTION IN HONOR OF ST. DYMPHNA

Virgin and Martyr

National Shrine of St. Dymphna, Massillon State Hospital, Massillon, Ohio

NATIONAL SHRINE OF ST. DYMPHNA

First Church in America dedicated
in her honor.

DEVOTION IN HONOR OF ST. DYMPHNA

Virgin and Martyr

(The Original Novena)

Patroness of Those Afflicted With

Mental and Nervous Disorders

Brief History of Her Life

(With Ecclesiastical Approbation)

Application for Membership
Pages 29 and 31

REV. MATTHEW M. HERTTNA

National Shrine of St. Dymphna
Massillon, Ohio

The beautiful Shrine of St. Dymphna on the grounds of the Massillon State Hospital was dedicated in honor of the Saint on her feast day, May 15th, 1939. It is the first Church in America to be built in honor of St. Dymphna and almost continuous novenas are being made in her honor.

The League of St. Dymphna is comprised of members throughout the country, whose intentions are remembered in the Masses and novenas here at the Shrine. A number of the members make the novena privately, asking that through her intercession they will be preserved from Mental and Nervous Disorders, or soon will recover if now afflicted.

Each week we receive many letters fro members of "The League of St. Dymphna' expressing gratitude that their prayers hav been answered through the intercession o this great Saint. May she ever continue t intercede for those who carry the crosses o nervous and mental suffering.

Father

PRAYER IN HONOR OF
ST. DYMPHNA

O GOD, Who gave St. Dymphna to Thy Infant Church in Brabant as a perfect model of virtue and didst deign that Thy servant seal with her innocent blood and with numerous miracles the teachings of the Holy Gospels so that the true religion might spread more rapidly, we beseech Thee that Thou wouldst grant especially to those who honor her reliques, Thy Protection, so that being fortified in the true faith and gratefully imitating all her virtues we may render greater glory to Thy Supreme and Infinite Majesty, through Jesus Christ Our Lord. Amen.

50 days Indulgence

Approved

+ EMMET M. WALSH,

Bishop of Youngstown

Nihil Obstat:

GEORGE M. DENNERLE,

Censor deputatus

Imprimatur:

† JAMES McFADDEN,

Bishop of Youngstown

May 11, 1936.

The Feast of St. Dymphna is celebrated
May 15th.

DEVOTION IN HONOR OF
ST. DYMPHNA

THE name of St. Dymphna is an object of veneration everywhere, but especially is it so in the city of Gheel, where the devotion to the saint is so natural to the inhabitants that it need not be aroused. The reason is of course evident. St. Dymphna dwelt in the city of Gheel until the time when she sanctified Gheelian soil by shedding her blood. Hers was the first shed for Jesus Christ and His Faith in Brabantine territory.

Sovereign Pontiffs and the Bishops have always shown their veneration for St. Dymphna and have favored with indulgences the church which is built over the saint's tomb; the tomb which God has favored with so many miracles through her intercession. Amidst such surroundings the people of Gheel cannot remain indifferent toward this holy virgin and martyr. In the older litanies St. Dymphna is mentioned not only under the title of Patroness of Gheel, but also as Patroness of Brabant.

The afflicted, who have invoked the name of St. Dymphna have not found her wanting. Since she resisted courageously the insane, raging love of her father, God has made her the special protectress of all who are afflicted with nervous disorders and the many miraculous cures at Gheel have established her in that title.

We ought to invoke the powerful aid of St. Dymphna with faith and confidence. We ought to celebrate her feast, honor her holy relics, attend the devotions held in her honor, and visit her Shrines. We ought to pray to her daily, and above all our younger generation ought to imitate her virtues, particularly her purity.

LITANY IN HONOR OF ST. DYMPHNA

Virgin and Martyr

Lord have mercy on us.
Christ have mercy on us.
Lord have mercy on us.
Christ hear us.
Christ graciously hear us.
God the Father of Heaven, *have mercy on us.*
God the Son, Redeemer of the world, *have mercy on us.*
God, the Holy Ghost, *have mercy on us.*
Holy Trinity, one God, *have mercy on us.*
Holy Mary, Virgin and Mother of God, conceived without sin, *pray for us,*
St. Dymphna, *pray for us.*
St. Dymphna, noble by birth but more noble in virtue,
St. Dymphna, docile to the lessons of your pious mother,
St. Dymphna, obedient to your saintly confessor, *Gerebran.*

Pray for us

St. Dymphna, who abandoned the court of your father, to escape the danger of impurity,

St. Dymphna, who chose a life of poverty on earth so that you might lay up treasure in Heaven,

St. Dymphna, who sought consolation in prayer and devout attendance of Holy Mass,

St. Dymphna, brilliant example of Christian youth,

St. Dymphna, who died a martyr, beheaded by your own father,

So that we may be humbled and obedient, placing no trust in ourselves,

So that we may carefully preserve the virtue of chastity according to our state by avoiding all dangerous occasions of sin.

So that we may persevere in our Faith,

So that we may learn to have confidence in the Lord during our afflictions.

Pray for us

So that we may obtain the spirit of prayer, the source of all graces,

So that we may love our Lord and God with all our heart and above all things,

So that we may receive the grace of final perseverance,

St. Dymphna, Patroness of Gheel,

St. Dymphna, Protectress against all nervous disorders,

St. Dymphna, consoler of the afflict-ed,

St. Dymphna, renowned for many miracles, particularly in Gheel,

In moments of temptation,

In times of contagious diseases, in time of war and persecution against the *faith,*

In our last *illness,*

At the hour of *death,*

Pray for us

Lamb of God, who takest away the sins of the world, *spare us, O Lord.*

Lamb of God, Who takest away the sins of the world, *graciously hear us, O Lord.*

Lamb of God, Who takest away the sins of the world, *have mercy on us.*

Christ hear us,
Christ graciously hear us.

Lord have mercy on us,
Christ have mercy on us,

Lord have mercy on us.

Our Father, etc.

Pray for us, St. Dymphna,

That we may be made worthy of the promises of Christ.

NOVENA IN HONOR OF ST. DYMPHNA

For preservation from nervous disorders through her intercession and for true wisdom through imitation of her virtues.

(During the novena the devotee should receive the sacraments of Penance and Holy Eucharist at least once.)

Let Us Pray

O God, Who gave St. Dymphna to the infant Church in Brabant as a model perfect in all virtues, and Who ordained that Thy handmaid should seal with her innocent blood and with numerous miracles the teachings of the Gospels for the spread of the true faith, grant we beseech Thee that those especially who honor the Holy Relics may continue to enjoy her powerful protection so that being fortified in faith and gratefully imitating her other virtues may be able to gain a new glory from Thy infinite and supreme majesty, through Christ our Lord. Amen.

FIRST DAY

Intention—Faith

O God, Source of our salvation, Who in the midst of a pagan people didst enlighten St. Dymphna by the true faith, which she professed under the guidance of her holy confessor, Gereberne, with such constancy that she suffered martyrdom, we beseech Thee through the intercession of these two saints that Thou wouldst deign to strengthen our faith which Thou hast given to us so that by wisely subjecting our souls to Thy Supreme Authority, and by faithfully regulating our lives by our faith we may honor Thee with our whole heart and soul until the hour of our death, through Jesus Christ, Our Lord. Amen.

Five times: Our Father, Hail Mary, Glory be to the Father.

SECOND DAY

Intention—Hope

O Almighty and Infinitely Good God, Who hast promised eternal salvation to those who obey Thy Commandments and profit by Thy grace, we beseech Thee, through the intercession of St. Dymphna, who fled from the danger of sin by quitting the palace of her father and who hoping thereby to gain eternal salvation fled to Brabant to live in poverty, grant that we also who are striving for eternal happiness may overcome all obstacles in the pathway of virtue and may attain eternal salvation through Jesus Christ, Our Lord. Amen.

Five times: Our Father, Hail Mary, Glory be to the Father.

THIRD DAY

Intention—Charity

O God of Love, Most Perfect Being, Creator of All That is Good and Beautiful, deign to help us by Thy powerful grace through the intercession of St. Dymphna, who in her youth loved Thee above all Creatures and loved her neighbor as herself for Thy Sake as the Image and Likeness of Thee, as the price of the Blood of Jesus and as co-heir of heaven, so that we may faithfully adhere to the two great commandments of charity not only in word, but in action and in truth, through Jesus Christ, Our Lord. Amen.

Five times: Our Father, Hail Mary, Glory be to the Father.

FOURTH DAY

Intention—Piety

O God, Our Creator and Supreme Master, we beseech Thee through the intercession of St. Dymphna, who served Thee with great zeal even in her childhood, hearing Thy word with great delight, assisting at Holy Mass with great respect, and receiving Holy Communion from the hand of St. Gerebran with tender devotion that Thou wouldst grant us the same virtue of piety so that having honored Thee during this life as our Creator we may possess Thee hereafter as our final reward through Jesus Christ, Our Lord. Amen.

Five times: Our Father, Hail Mary, Glory be to the Father.

FIFTH DAY

Intention—Prudence

O God, Ruler of the universe, Who allowed St. Dymphna to discover an efficacious means of avoiding the criminal intentions of her father, deign to grant through the merits of Thy Holy servant, that we may become simple as doves and wise as serpents so that through prudent advice and sound judgment we may perceive that which is t be avoided and that which is to b followed in order to happily achieve th great work of our salvation throug Jesus Christ, Our Lord. Amen.

Five times: Our Father, Hail Mary, Glory be to the Father.

SIXTH DAY

Intention—Justice

O God, Source of eternal justice, we supplicate Thee through the intercession of St. Dymphna, who in order to render to Thee that which is Thine, fled from her country and her father, that Thou wouldst deign to make us seek after justice so that we may perform rightly our duties toward Thee as we see them, through Jesus Christ, Our Lord. Amen.

Five times: Our Father, Hail Mary, Glory be to the Father.

SEVENTH DAY

Intention—Fortitude

O God, rewarder of those who remain firm in their good resolutions, we beseech Thee through the meditation of the merits of St. Dymphna, who through love of virtue had the courage to suffer privation, persecution and even martyredom, that Thou wouldst grant us fortitude so that we may courageously and perseveringly overcome ourselves and finally conquer the enemy of our salvation through Jesus Christ, Our Lord. Amen.

Five times: Our Father, Hail Mary, Glory be to the Father.

EIGHTH DAY

Intention—Temperance

O God, who hast made St. Dymphna resplendent in the virtue of temperance so that she mastered sensual inclination and tempered the use of earthly goods, uniting with this the beautiful virtues of modesty, docility and humility which is called the foundation of all virtue because humility banishes from the soul pride which is an obstacle to grace, we beseech Thee through the intercession of St. Dymphna that Thou wouldst deign to guide and direct us so that being preserved from all nervous disorders we may come to a happy end in the good counsels Thou hast given through Jesus Christ, Our Lord. Amen.

Five times: Our Father, Hail Mary, Glory be to the Father.

NINTH DAY

Intention—Chastity

O God, Lover of innocent souls, Who gave to St. Dymphna the virtue of angelic purity which rendered her reserved in all her actions, so modest in her dress, so attentive in her conversation, so circumspect in her bearing that she shed her blood to preserve this precious virtue, we beseech Thee that Thou bestow upon us the virtue of chastity so that we may enjoy peace of conscience in this life and the pure eternal joys of heaven hereafter through Jesus Christ, Our Lord. Amen.

Five times: Our Father, Hail Mary, Glory be to the Father.

These Prayers In The Form Of A Novena Were Approved By Pope Urban VIII In 1635

A Brief Story of St. Dymphna, Patron of Victims of Nervous, Mental Disorders*

∫

The success of the Colony of Gheel, Belgium, all these years can be attributed to the intercession of St. Dymphna.

*Reprint from Tabernacle and Purgatory, published by Benedictine Convent Sisters, Clyde, Mo., May, 1946.

St. Dymphna, Patroness of Those Afflicted with Nervous and Mental Disorders

ISLE OF SAINTS" has long been a title popularly given to the island evangelized by St. Patrick, which nestles in the blue waters of the Atlantic. And appropriately it is so called, for the names of the Irish saints would more than fill the Church's calendar. Yet it is to be regretted that Catholics for the most part are entirely unfamiliar with so many of these glorious saints, yes, even ignorant of their very names. One such forgotten or unknown saint, who, on account of her spotless virtue and glorious martyrdom, is sometimes referred to as the "Lily of Eire," is St. Dymphna. True, the records of the life and martyrdom of this holy virgin are for the most part meagre and unsatisfactory, but sufficient is known regarding the principal facts of her life and of her many well-authenticated miracles to attest to an exalted sanctity.

St. Dymphna was born in the 7th century, when Ireland was almost universally Catholic. Yet, strange to say, her father, a petty king of Oriel, was still a pagan. Her mother, a descendant of a noble family, was, on the other hand, a devout Christian, who was remarkable both for her piety and her great beauty. Dymphna was, like her mother, a paragon of beauty, and a most sweet and winning child, the "jewel" of her home. Every affection and attention was lavished upon her from birth. Heaven, too, favored the child with special graces. Dymphna was early placed under the care and tutelage of a pious Christian woman, who prepared her for baptism, which was conferred by the saintly priest Father Gerebran. The latter seems to have been a member of the household, and later taught little Dymphna her letters along with the truths of religion. Dymphna was a bright and eager pupil, and advanced rapidly in wisdom and grace. When still very young, Dymphna, like so many other noble Irish maidens before and after her, being filled with fervor and love for Jesus Christ, chose Him for her Divine Spouse and consecrated her virginity to Him and to His Blessed Mother by a vow of chastity.

It was not long, however, until an unexpected cloud overshadowed the happy childhood of the beautiful girl. She lost her good mother by death. Many were the secret tears she shed over this bereavement, but at the same time she found great comfort in the Divine Faith which, though she was still of tender age, already had taken deep root.

Dymphna's father, too, greatly mourned his deceased wife and for a long time continued prostrate with grief. At length he was persuaded by his counsellors to seek solace in a second marriage. So he commissioned certain ones of his court to seek out for him a lady who would be like his first spouse in beauty and character. After visiting many countries in vain, the messengers returned saying that they could find none so charming and amiable as his own lovely daughter, Dymphna. Giving ear to their base suggestion, the king conceived the evil design of marrying Dymphna. With persuasive and flattering words he manifested his purpose to her. Dymphna, as may be expected, was greatly horrified at the suggestion, and asked for a period of forty days to consider the proposal. She immediately betook herself to Father Gerebran, who advised her to flee from her native country, and since the danger was imminent, he urged her to make no delay.

With all speed, therefore, she set out for the continent, accompanied by Father Gerebran, the court jester and his wife. After a favorable passage, they arrived on the coast near the present city of Antwerp. Having stopped for a short rest, they resumed their journey and came to a little village named Gheel. Here they were hospitably received and began to make plans for establishing their future abode at the place.

The king, in the meantime, having discovered Dymphna's flight, was fearfully angry and immediately set out with his followers in search of the fugitives. After some time, they were traced to Belgium and their place of refuge was located. At first, Dymphna's father tried to persuade her to return with him, but Father Gerebran sternly rebuked him for his wicked intentions, whereupon he gave orders that Father Gerebran should be put to death. Without delay, his wicked retainers laid violent hands upon the priest and struck him on the neck with a sword. With one blow of the steel the head was severed from the shoulders and another glorious martyr went to join the illustrious heroes of Christ's kingdom.

Further attempts on the part of Dymphna's father to induce her to return with him proved fruitless. With undaunted courage she spurned his enticing promises and scorned his cruel threats. Infuriated by her resistance, the father drew a dagger from his belt and he himself struck off the head of his child. Recommending her soul to the mercy of God. the holy virgin fell prostrate at the feet of her insanely raving father. Thus the glorious crown of martyrdom was accorded to St. Dymphna in the fifteenth year of her age, on the fifteenth day of May, between 620 and 640. The day of her death has been assigned as her feastday.

The records of Dymphna's life and death say that the bodies of the two martyred saints lay on the ground for quite some time after their death, until the inhabitants of Gheel removed them to a cave, which was the customary manner of interment in that part of the world at the time of the martyrdoms. But after several years had elapsed, the villagers, recalling their holy deaths, decided to give the bodies a more suitable burial. When the workmen removed the heap of black earth at the cave's entrance, great was their astonishment to find two most beautiful tombs, whiter than snow, which were carved from stone, as if by angel hands. When the coffin of St. Dymphna was opened there was found lying on her breast a red tile bearing the inscription: "Here lies the holy virgin and martyr, Dymphna." The remains of the saint were placed in a small church. Later necessity obliged the erection of the magnificent "Church of St. Dymphna" which now stands on the site where the bodies were first buried. St. Dymphna's relics repose there in a beautiful golden reliquary.

Miracles and cures began to occur in continually increasing numbers. Gradually St. Dymphna's fame as patroness of victims of nervous diseases and mental disorders was spread from country to country. More and more mentally afflicted persons were brought to the shrine by relatives and friends, many coming in pilgrimages from far-distant places. Novenas were made, and St. Dymphna's relic was applied to the patients. The remarkable cures reported caused confidence in the saint to grow daily. At first the patients were lodged in a small annex built onto the church. Then gradually it came about that the patients were placed in the homes of the families living in Gheel. From this beginning Gheel developed into a town world-famed for its care of the insane and mentally afflicted. An institution, called the "Infirmary of St. Elizabeth," which was conducted by the Sisters of St. Augustine was later built for the hospital care of the patients. Most of the latter, after some time spent in the institution, are placed in one or other of the families of Gheel, where they lead a comparatively normal life. Every home in Gheel is proud to welcome to its inmost family circle such patients as are ready to return to the environment of family life. Generations of experience have given to the people of Gheel an intimate and tender skill in dealing with their charges, and their remarkable spirit of charity and Christlike love for these afflicted members of society gives to our modern-day world, so prone to put its whole reliance on science and to forget the principles of true Christian charity, a lesson the practice of which would do much to restore certain types of mentally afflicted individuals to an almost normal outlook on life.

Renowned psychiatrists are in full agreement with this statement, and testify that a surprisingly large number of patients could leave mental institutions if they could be assured of a sympathetic reception in the world, such as the people of Gheel take pride in showing. In fact, psychiatrists state that institutions can help certain cases only to a given extent, and when that point is reached, they must have help from persons outside the institution if the progress made in the institution is to have fruition. Gheel is the living confirmation of this statement and an exemplar of the Gospel teachings on charity.

Further information about the Saint and the League, pictures, prayers and statues, may be obtained from:

REV. M. M. HERTTNA
National Shrine of St. Dymphna
Massillon, Ohio

Application for Membership

in

THE LEAGUE OF SAINT DYMPHNA

Established by His Excellency,
Most Rev. James A. McFadden

To care for the spiritual needs of those troubled with mental and nervous disorders

Dues .... $1.00 Per Year, per person
Perpetual membership $25.00

Either living or deceased persons may be enrolled as members and thereby share in the numerous benefits of this League.

Spiritual Benefits are:

High Mass offered each week for the living members of the League.

High Mass offered each week for the deceased members of the League.

Mass is offered for the repose of the Soul of all members who die and notice of their death sent to the Chaplain.

A remembrance in the Novena prayers of the patients and all members.

Why not enroll your family and friends under the protection of this great Saint and thereby enlist her aid in preserving us all from nervous disorders?

NAME ....

ADDRESS ....

CITY .... STATE ....

Application for Membership
in
THE LEAGUE OF SAINT DYMPHNA

Established by His Excellency,
Most Rev. James A. McFadden

To care for the spiritual needs of those troubled with mental and nervous disorders

Dues .... $1.00 Per Year, per person

Perpetual membership $25.00

Either living or deceased persons may be enrolled as members and thereby share in the numerous benefits of this League.

Spiritual Benefits are:

High Mass offered each week for the living members of the League.

High Mass offered each week for the deceased members of the League.

Mass is offered for the repose of the Soul of all members who die and notice of their death sent to the Chaplain.

A remembrance in the Novena prayers of the patients and all members.

Why not enroll your family and friends under the protection of this great Saint and thereby enlist her aid in preserving us all from nervous disorders?

NAME ....

ADDRESS ....

CITY................................... STATE ....

Additional names may be added on reverse side.